50 Every Season Recipes for Home

By: Kelly Johnson

Table of Contents

- Spring Asparagus and Lemon Risotto
- Summer Corn and Tomato Salad
- Fall Butternut Squash Soup
- Winter Root Vegetable Stew
- Spring Strawberry Spinach Salad
- Summer Grilled Peaches with Honey
- Fall Apple Cinnamon Oatmeal
- Winter Beef and Barley Soup
- Spring Herb-Crusted Salmon
- Summer Caprese Pasta
- Fall Pumpkin Spice Muffins
- Winter Baked Ziti
- Spring Green Goddess Quinoa Bowl
- Summer Watermelon Feta Salad
- Fall Sweet Potato and Black Bean Tacos
- Winter Chicken Pot Pie
- Spring Radish and Cucumber Salad
- Summer BBQ Pulled Pork Sandwiches
- Fall Maple Glazed Brussels Sprouts
- Winter Creamy Tomato Soup
- Spring Lemon Garlic Shrimp
- Summer Gazpacho
- Fall Roasted Apple and Butternut Squash Salad
- Winter Sausage and Kale Soup
- Spring Pea and Mint Pesto Pasta
- Summer Grilled Chicken Caesar Salad
- Fall Spiced Apple Cider
- Winter Beef Stroganoff
- Spring Roasted Beet Salad
- Summer Mango Salsa
- Fall Pumpkin Ravioli
- Winter Cozy Chili
- Spring Avocado and Black Bean Tacos
- Summer Zucchini Noodles with Pesto
- Fall Pear and Gorgonzola Salad
- Winter Garlic Parmesan Roasted Potatoes

- Spring Carrot and Ginger Soup
- Summer Lobster Rolls
- Fall Cranberry Walnut Bread
- Winter Creamy Mushroom Risotto
- Spring Artichoke and Lemon Pasta
- Summer Grilled Vegetable Platter
- Fall Baked Apples with Cinnamon
- Winter Spinach and Feta Stuffed Chicken
- Spring Roasted Lemon Herb Chicken
- Summer Thai Beef Salad
- Fall Acorn Squash with Maple Glaze
- Winter Sweet Potato Shepherd's Pie
- Spring Chickpea and Avocado Salad
- Summer Strawberry Shortcake

Spring Asparagus and Lemon Risotto

Ingredients:

- **1 bunch asparagus** (about 1 pound, trimmed and cut into 1-inch pieces)
- **4 cups chicken or vegetable broth** (low sodium)
- **2 tablespoons olive oil**
- **1 small onion** (finely chopped)
- **2 cloves garlic** (minced)
- **1 1/2 cups Arborio rice**
- **1/2 cup dry white wine**
- **1/2 cup grated Parmesan cheese**
- **1 tablespoon lemon zest** (about 1 lemon)
- **2 tablespoons fresh lemon juice** (about 1 lemon)
- **Salt and black pepper** (to taste)
- **1/4 cup fresh parsley** (chopped, for garnish)

Instructions:

1. **Prepare the Asparagus:**
    - Bring a pot of salted water to a boil. Add the asparagus pieces and cook for about 2 minutes until tender-crisp. Drain and transfer to a bowl of ice water to stop the cooking process. Drain again and set aside.
2. **Heat the Broth:**
    - In a saucepan, heat the chicken or vegetable broth over low heat. Keep it warm but not boiling.
3. **Sauté the Aromatics:**
    - In a large skillet or Dutch oven, heat the olive oil over medium heat. Add the chopped onion and cook until softened and translucent, about 4-5 minutes.
    - Add the minced garlic and cook for another 1-2 minutes, until fragrant.
4. **Toast the Rice:**
    - Stir in the Arborio rice and cook for 1-2 minutes, allowing the rice to lightly toast and absorb the flavors.
5. **Deglaze with Wine:**
    - Pour in the white wine and cook, stirring constantly, until the wine is mostly absorbed by the rice.
6. **Add the Broth:**
    - Begin adding the warm broth to the rice one ladleful at a time. Stir frequently and allow each addition of broth to be absorbed before adding the next. This process will take about 18-20 minutes.
7. **Incorporate the Asparagus:**
    - When the rice is creamy and tender but still slightly al dente, gently fold in the cooked asparagus pieces.
8. **Finish the Risotto:**

- Stir in the grated Parmesan cheese, lemon zest, and lemon juice. Season with salt and black pepper to taste.
9. **Serve:**
    - Garnish with fresh parsley and serve immediately

Tips:

- **Stirring:** Frequent stirring helps release the rice's starch, which contributes to the creamy texture of the risotto.
- **Consistency:** The risotto should be creamy and slightly loose; it will continue to thicken as it sits.
- **Wine:** If you prefer not to use wine, you can substitute with an additional 1/2 cup of broth and a splash of white wine vinegar or lemon juice for acidity.

Spring Asparagus and Lemon Risotto is a light, yet satisfying dish that beautifully showcases the flavors of spring. Enjoy this risotto as a main course or alongside grilled chicken or seafood for a complete meal.

Summer Corn and Tomato Salad

Ingredients:

- **4 cups fresh corn kernels** (about 4 ears of corn, husked and kernels removed)
- **2 cups cherry or grape tomatoes** (halved)
- **1/2 red onion** (finely chopped)
- **1/4 cup fresh basil leaves** (chopped)
- **1/4 cup fresh parsley leaves** (chopped)
- **1/4 cup crumbled feta cheese** (optional)

For the Dressing:

- **3 tablespoons olive oil**
- **2 tablespoons red wine vinegar** (or lemon juice)
- **1 teaspoon honey** (or maple syrup)
- **1 clove garlic** (minced)
- **Salt and black pepper** (to taste)

Instructions:

1. **Cook the Corn:**
   - Bring a large pot of salted water to a boil. Add the corn kernels and cook for about 2-3 minutes until just tender.
   - Drain the corn and immediately transfer it to a bowl of ice water to stop the cooking process. Drain again and set aside.
2. **Prepare the Vegetables:**
   - In a large bowl, combine the cooked corn, cherry or grape tomatoes, and finely chopped red onion.
3. **Make the Dressing:**
   - In a small bowl or jar, whisk together the olive oil, red wine vinegar (or lemon juice), honey, minced garlic, salt, and black pepper.
4. **Combine and Toss:**
   - Pour the dressing over the corn and tomato mixture. Toss gently to coat all the ingredients evenly.
5. **Add Herbs and Cheese:**
   - Fold in the chopped basil, parsley, and crumbled feta cheese (if using).
6. **Chill and Serve:**
   - Let the salad sit for at least 15 minutes to allow the flavors to meld. Serve chilled or at room temperature.

Tips:

- **Corn:** For extra sweetness, you can grill the corn before removing the kernels. Simply brush with oil and grill until slightly charred.

- **Tomatoes:** Use a variety of cherry or grape tomatoes for different flavors and colors.
- **Cheese:** If you prefer, you can substitute feta cheese with goat cheese or omit it for a dairy-free version.
- **Herbs:** Fresh herbs are key for flavor, but you can also experiment with mint or cilantro.

Summer Corn and Tomato Salad is a refreshing and versatile dish that's perfect for barbecues, picnics, or as a light meal on its own. Enjoy the bright, summery flavors!

Fall Butternut Squash Soup

Ingredients:

- **1 large butternut squash** (peeled, seeded, and cubed, about 4 cups)
- **2 tablespoons olive oil**
- **1 medium onion** (chopped)
- **2 cloves garlic** (minced)
- **1 large carrot** (peeled and chopped)
- **2 celery stalks** (chopped)
- **4 cups vegetable or chicken broth**
- **1/2 cup canned coconut milk** (or heavy cream)
- **1 teaspoon ground cumin**
- **1/2 teaspoon ground cinnamon**
- **1/4 teaspoon ground nutmeg**
- **1/4 teaspoon ground ginger**
- **Salt and black pepper** (to taste)
- **1-2 tablespoons maple syrup** (optional, for added sweetness)
- **Fresh parsley or chives** (for garnish)
- **Croutons or toasted pumpkin seeds** (optional, for topping)

Instructions:

1. **Roast the Butternut Squash:**
   - Preheat your oven to 400°F (200°C).
   - Toss the butternut squash cubes with 1 tablespoon of olive oil, salt, and pepper. Spread them in a single layer on a baking sheet.
   - Roast for 25-30 minutes, or until the squash is tender and caramelized, turning halfway through.
2. **Sauté the Aromatics:**
   - In a large pot, heat the remaining 1 tablespoon of olive oil over medium heat.
   - Add the chopped onion, carrot, and celery. Cook, stirring occasionally, until the vegetables are softened, about 5-7 minutes.
   - Add the minced garlic and cook for another 1-2 minutes, until fragrant.
3. **Combine and Cook:**
   - Add the roasted butternut squash to the pot with the sautéed vegetables.
   - Stir in the ground cumin, cinnamon, nutmeg, and ginger. Cook for 1-2 minutes to allow the spices to become fragrant.
4. **Add Broth:**
   - Pour in the vegetable or chicken broth and bring the mixture to a simmer. Cook for 10-15 minutes to blend the flavors.
5. **Blend the Soup:**
   - Use an immersion blender to purée the soup until smooth. Alternatively, carefully transfer the soup in batches to a blender and blend until smooth. Return the soup to the pot.

6. **Finish the Soup:**
   - Stir in the coconut milk (or heavy cream) and maple syrup if using. Adjust seasoning with salt and black pepper to taste.
   - Heat the soup over low heat until warmed through.
7. **Serve:**
   - Ladle the soup into bowls and garnish with fresh parsley or chives. Top with croutons or toasted pumpkin seeds if desired.

Tips:

- **Roasting:** Roasting the squash caramelizes its natural sugars and enhances its flavor. Don't skip this step for the best results.
- **Blending:** For an ultra-smooth texture, ensure you blend the soup thoroughly. An immersion blender is convenient for this.
- **Sweetness:** Adjust the sweetness with maple syrup according to your taste. Some butternut squash varieties are naturally sweeter than others.

Fall Butternut Squash Soup is a cozy, nutritious dish that's ideal for chilly days. Its rich, velvety texture and warm spices make it a comforting favorite for the season.

Winter Root Vegetable Stew

Ingredients:

- **2 tablespoons olive oil**
- **1 large onion** (chopped)
- **3 cloves garlic** (minced)
- **3 large carrots** (peeled and chopped)
- **2 parsnips** (peeled and chopped)
- **1 large rutabaga** (peeled and chopped)
- **2 medium potatoes** (peeled and chopped)
- **1 cup celery** (chopped)
- **1 cup turnips** (peeled and chopped, optional)
- **4 cups vegetable or beef broth**
- **1 cup diced tomatoes** (canned or fresh)
- **2 tablespoons tomato paste**
- **1 teaspoon dried thyme**
- **1 teaspoon dried rosemary**
- **1/2 teaspoon ground cumin**
- **1 bay leaf**
- **Salt and black pepper** (to taste)
- **1 cup frozen peas** (optional, for added color and sweetness)
- **Fresh parsley** (chopped, for garnish)

Instructions:

1. **Sauté the Aromatics:**
    - In a large pot or Dutch oven, heat the olive oil over medium heat.
    - Add the chopped onion and cook until softened and translucent, about 5 minutes.
    - Add the minced garlic and cook for another 1-2 minutes, until fragrant.
2. **Add the Vegetables:**
    - Stir in the carrots, parsnips, rutabaga, potatoes, celery, and turnips (if using). Cook for about 5-7 minutes, stirring occasionally.
3. **Incorporate the Broth and Seasonings:**
    - Add the vegetable or beef broth, diced tomatoes, tomato paste, dried thyme, rosemary, ground cumin, and bay leaf. Stir well to combine.
    - Bring the mixture to a boil, then reduce the heat to low and simmer, uncovered, for about 30-40 minutes, or until the vegetables are tender.
4. **Add Peas and Adjust Seasoning:**
    - If using, stir in the frozen peas and cook for an additional 5 minutes.
    - Remove the bay leaf and season the stew with salt and black pepper to taste.
5. **Serve:**
    - Ladle the stew into bowls and garnish with chopped fresh parsley.

Tips:

- **Vegetable Variety:** Feel free to mix and match root vegetables based on what's available or your preferences. Sweet potatoes or turnips can also be good additions.
- **Thickening:** If you prefer a thicker stew, you can mash some of the vegetables with a spoon or use a potato masher to break down a portion of the stew.
- **Make Ahead:** This stew can be made ahead of time and stored in the refrigerator for up to 3 days. It also freezes well for up to 3 months.

Winter Root Vegetable Stew is a comforting and filling meal that's perfect for cold winter days. Its rich flavors and hearty texture make it a satisfying dish for any winter meal.

Spring Strawberry Spinach Salad

Ingredients:

- **4 cups baby spinach** (washed and dried)
- **1 pint fresh strawberries** (hulled and sliced)
- **1/4 cup red onion** (thinly sliced)
- **1/4 cup crumbled feta cheese** (or goat cheese)
- **1/4 cup sliced almonds** (toasted)
- **1/4 cup candied pecans** (or walnuts, optional)
- **1/4 cup balsamic vinaigrette** (or your favorite dressing)

For the Balsamic Vinaigrette (if making homemade):

- **1/4 cup balsamic vinegar**
- **2 tablespoons honey** (or maple syrup)
- **1/2 cup extra-virgin olive oil**
- **1 teaspoon Dijon mustard**
- **Salt and black pepper** (to taste)

Instructions:

1. **Prepare the Ingredients:**
   - Wash and dry the baby spinach. Hull and slice the strawberries. Thinly slice the red onion.
2. **Toast the Nuts:**
   - In a small skillet over medium heat, toast the sliced almonds until golden and fragrant, about 2-3 minutes. Be careful not to burn them. Remove from heat and let cool.
3. **Make the Vinaigrette (if using homemade):**
   - In a small bowl or jar, whisk together the balsamic vinegar, honey, Dijon mustard, salt, and black pepper.
   - Slowly whisk in the olive oil until the dressing is well combined and emulsified.
4. **Assemble the Salad:**
   - In a large salad bowl, combine the baby spinach, sliced strawberries, and red onion.
   - Add the crumbled feta cheese, toasted almonds, and candied pecans (if using).
5. **Dress the Salad:**
   - Drizzle the balsamic vinaigrette over the salad and toss gently to coat all the ingredients.
6. **Serve:**
   - Serve immediately for the freshest taste, or chill in the refrigerator for up to 30 minutes before serving.

Tips:

- **Sweetness:** Adjust the amount of honey or maple syrup in the vinaigrette to match your taste preference.
- **Nuts:** Feel free to substitute other nuts like walnuts or pecans if you prefer.
- **Cheese:** If you're not a fan of feta or goat cheese, you can use another cheese like Parmesan or omit it entirely.

Spring Strawberry Spinach Salad is a delightful combination of sweet, tangy, and savory flavors that's perfect for a light lunch or as a refreshing side dish. Enjoy the vibrant tastes of spring with this easy-to-make salad!

Summer Grilled Peaches with Honey

Ingredients:

- **4 ripe peaches** (halved and pitted)
- **2 tablespoons olive oil** (or melted butter)
- **2 tablespoons honey** (or more, to taste)
- **1/2 teaspoon ground cinnamon** (optional)
- **Fresh mint leaves** (for garnish, optional)
- **Vanilla ice cream or Greek yogurt** (optional, for serving)

Instructions:

1. **Prepare the Peaches:**
   - Preheat your grill to medium-high heat.
   - Brush the cut sides of the peaches with olive oil or melted butter to prevent sticking.
2. **Grill the Peaches:**
   - Place the peach halves cut side down on the grill.
   - Grill for about 4-5 minutes, or until grill marks appear and the peaches are slightly softened.
   - Flip the peaches and grill for an additional 2-3 minutes on the skin side.
3. **Add Cinnamon (Optional):**
   - If using, sprinkle ground cinnamon over the peaches during the last minute of grilling for added flavor.
4. **Drizzle with Honey:**
   - Remove the peaches from the grill and transfer to a serving platter.
   - Drizzle honey over the grilled peaches while they are still warm.
5. **Garnish and Serve:**
   - Garnish with fresh mint leaves if desired.
   - Serve the grilled peaches warm on their own or with a scoop of vanilla ice cream or a dollop of Greek yogurt for an extra treat.

Tips:

- **Peach Ripeness:** Use ripe but firm peaches for grilling. Overripe peaches can become mushy.
- **Grill Marks:** For more pronounced grill marks, make sure the grill grates are clean and well-oiled.
- **Flavor Variations:** Try adding a sprinkle of sea salt or a dash of nutmeg for additional flavor.

Summer Grilled Peaches with Honey is an easy and elegant dessert that takes advantage of the season's fresh produce. The combination of caramelized peaches and sweet honey is simply irresistible!

Fall Apple Cinnamon Oatmeal

Ingredients:

- **1 cup old-fashioned rolled oats**
- **2 cups milk** (or a dairy-free alternative such as almond, soy, or oat milk)
- **1 large apple** (peeled, cored, and diced)
- **1 tablespoon brown sugar** (or maple syrup/honey, to taste)
- **1 teaspoon ground cinnamon**
- **1/4 teaspoon ground nutmeg** (optional)
- **1/4 teaspoon vanilla extract**
- **Pinch of salt**
- **1/4 cup chopped nuts** (such as walnuts or pecans, optional)
- **1/4 cup raisins or dried cranberries** (optional)
- **Fresh apple slices** (for garnish, optional)
- **Additional milk or sweetener** (for serving, optional)

Instructions:

1. **Cook the Apples:**
    - In a medium saucepan, combine the diced apples with 1/4 cup of water and cook over medium heat for about 5 minutes, or until the apples are tender. Stir occasionally.
2. **Prepare the Oats:**
    - In a separate saucepan, bring the milk to a boil over medium-high heat.
    - Stir in the rolled oats, brown sugar (or maple syrup/honey), ground cinnamon, nutmeg (if using), and a pinch of salt.
3. **Simmer the Oatmeal:**
    - Reduce the heat to low and simmer, stirring occasionally, for about 5-7 minutes, or until the oats are cooked and have absorbed most of the liquid.
4. **Combine Ingredients:**
    - Fold the cooked apples into the oatmeal and stir to combine. Cook for an additional 1-2 minutes to allow the flavors to meld.
5. **Add Extras (Optional):**
    - Stir in the chopped nuts and raisins or dried cranberries if desired.
6. **Serve:**
    - Spoon the oatmeal into bowls. Garnish with fresh apple slices and a drizzle of additional milk or a bit more sweetener if desired.

Tips:

- **Consistency:** Adjust the consistency of the oatmeal by adding more milk if you prefer a creamier texture.
- **Sweetness:** Taste and adjust the sweetness to your liking, adding more brown sugar or maple syrup as needed.

- **Toppings:** Feel free to top with other seasonal fruits or a sprinkle of additional cinnamon for extra flavor.

Fall Apple Cinnamon Oatmeal is a delightful breakfast that brings together the flavors of the season in a warm and satisfying way. Enjoy it as a cozy start to your day or as a comforting meal anytime you crave a touch of autumn!

Winter Beef and Barley Soup

Ingredients:

- 2 tablespoons olive oil
- 1 lb beef stew meat (cut into 1-inch cubes)
- 1 large onion (chopped)
- 3 cloves garlic (minced)
- 3 large carrots (peeled and sliced)
- 2 celery stalks (chopped)
- 1 cup pearl barley (rinsed)
- 4 cups beef broth
- 2 cups water (or more as needed)
- 1 cup diced tomatoes (canned or fresh)
- 1 teaspoon dried thyme
- 1 teaspoon dried rosemary
- 2 bay leaves
- Salt and black pepper (to taste)
- 1 cup frozen peas (optional)
- 1 cup chopped kale or spinach (optional, for added greens)

Instructions:

1. **Brown the Beef:**
    - In a large pot or Dutch oven, heat the olive oil over medium-high heat.
    - Add the beef stew meat and cook until browned on all sides, about 5-7 minutes. Remove the beef from the pot and set aside.
2. **Sauté the Vegetables:**
    - In the same pot, add the chopped onion, carrots, and celery. Cook until the vegetables are softened, about 5 minutes.
    - Add the minced garlic and cook for an additional 1 minute, until fragrant.
3. **Add the Barley and Broth:**
    - Stir in the pearl barley, then return the browned beef to the pot.
    - Add the beef broth, water, diced tomatoes, dried thyme, rosemary, and bay leaves. Stir to combine.
4. **Simmer the Soup:**
    - Bring the soup to a boil, then reduce the heat to low and simmer, uncovered, for about 45-60 minutes, or until the beef is tender and the barley is cooked. Stir occasionally.
5. **Add Optional Ingredients:**
    - If using, stir in the frozen peas and chopped kale or spinach during the last 10 minutes of cooking. Adjust the seasoning with salt and black pepper to taste.
6. **Serve:**
    - Remove the bay leaves before serving.
    - Ladle the soup into bowls and serve hot.

Tips:

- **Beef:** Use a cut of beef suitable for stewing, such as chuck or round, for best results.
- **Barley:** Pearl barley works well for this recipe. If you prefer a quicker-cooking option, you can use quick-cooking barley.
- **Thickness:** If you prefer a thicker soup, you can mash some of the vegetables or use an immersion blender to partially blend the soup.

Winter Beef and Barley Soup is a robust and nourishing meal that's perfect for warming up on chilly winter days. It's easy to make, packed with flavor, and provides comfort and satisfaction in every bowl. Enjoy!

Spring Herb-Crusted Salmon

Ingredients:

- **4 salmon fillets** (6 oz each, skin-on or skinless)
- **1/2 cup fresh parsley** (chopped)
- **1/4 cup fresh dill** (chopped)
- **1/4 cup fresh chives** (chopped)
- **1/4 cup breadcrumbs** (preferably whole wheat or panko)
- **2 tablespoons Dijon mustard**
- **2 tablespoons olive oil**
- **1 lemon** (zested and juiced)
- **2 cloves garlic** (minced)
- **Salt and black pepper** (to taste)
- **Lemon wedges** (for serving)

Instructions:

1. **Preheat the Oven:**
   - Preheat your oven to 375°F (190°C). Line a baking sheet with parchment paper or lightly grease it.
2. **Prepare the Herb Mixture:**
   - In a small bowl, combine the chopped parsley, dill, chives, breadcrumbs, and minced garlic. Mix well.
3. **Season the Salmon:**
   - Pat the salmon fillets dry with paper towels. Season both sides with salt and black pepper.
   - Place the salmon fillets on the prepared baking sheet.
4. **Apply the Mustard Mixture:**
   - In a small bowl, whisk together the Dijon mustard, olive oil, lemon zest, and lemon juice.
   - Spread a thin layer of the mustard mixture over the top of each salmon fillet.
5. **Add the Herb Crust:**
   - Press the herb and breadcrumb mixture onto the mustard-coated side of each salmon fillet, ensuring an even coating.
6. **Bake the Salmon:**
   - Bake in the preheated oven for 15-20 minutes, or until the salmon is cooked through and flakes easily with a fork. The crust should be golden brown and crispy.
7. **Serve:**
   - Serve the herb-crusted salmon with lemon wedges on the side for extra brightness. Accompany with your favorite spring vegetables or a light salad.

Tips:

- **Salmon Freshness:** Use fresh, high-quality salmon for the best flavor and texture.
- **Herb Variations:** Feel free to mix and match herbs based on what's available or to suit your taste preferences.
- **Crispier Crust:** For an extra crispy crust, you can broil the salmon for the last 2-3 minutes of cooking.

Spring Herb-Crusted Salmon is a delightful way to enjoy the fresh flavors of spring. It pairs beautifully with seasonal vegetables and is a light yet satisfying option for any meal. Enjoy this delicious and healthy dish!

Summer Caprese Pasta

Ingredients:

- **12 oz pasta** (such as penne, fusilli, or farfalle)
- **2 cups cherry or grape tomatoes** (halved)
- **8 oz fresh mozzarella balls** (or 1 cup of diced mozzarella)
- **1/4 cup fresh basil leaves** (chopped)
- **3 tablespoons extra-virgin olive oil**
- **2 tablespoons balsamic glaze** (optional, for drizzling)
- **1 clove garlic** (minced)
- **Salt and black pepper** (to taste)
- **1/4 cup grated Parmesan cheese** (optional, for serving)

Instructions:

1. **Cook the Pasta:**
    - Bring a large pot of salted water to a boil. Add the pasta and cook according to the package instructions until al dente.
    - Drain the pasta and set aside. Reserve a small cup of pasta water.
2. **Prepare the Tomatoes and Garlic:**
    - While the pasta is cooking, heat 2 tablespoons of olive oil in a large skillet over medium heat.
    - Add the minced garlic and cook for about 1 minute, until fragrant. Be careful not to burn it.
    - Add the halved cherry or grape tomatoes and cook for 3-4 minutes, just until they start to soften and release their juices. Season with salt and black pepper.
3. **Combine Ingredients:**
    - Add the cooked pasta to the skillet with the tomatoes. Toss to combine.
    - If the mixture seems dry, add a bit of the reserved pasta water, 1 tablespoon at a time, until you reach your desired consistency.
4. **Add Mozzarella and Basil:**
    - Remove the skillet from heat and stir in the fresh mozzarella and chopped basil.
    - Drizzle with the remaining 1 tablespoon of olive oil and toss gently to combine.
5. **Serve:**
    - Transfer the pasta to serving dishes. If desired, drizzle with balsamic glaze for extra flavor.
    - Garnish with grated Parmesan cheese, if using.

Tips:

- **Tomato Variety:** You can use any type of ripe tomato. Cherry or grape tomatoes are ideal for their sweetness and convenience.
- **Mozzarella:** Fresh mozzarella adds a creamy texture, but you can use regular mozzarella if that's what you have on hand.

- **Balsamic Glaze:** If you don't have balsamic glaze, you can use regular balsamic vinegar, but drizzle it lightly to avoid overpowering the dish.

Summer Caprese Pasta is a fresh and delightful dish that brings the essence of summer to your table. It's perfect for a quick lunch or a light dinner, and it celebrates the best of seasonal ingredients. Enjoy this easy and delicious pasta recipe!

Fall Pumpkin Spice Muffins

Ingredients:

- 1 1/2 cups all-purpose flour
- 1 cup canned pumpkin puree (not pumpkin pie filling)
- 1/2 cup granulated sugar
- 1/2 cup packed brown sugar
- 1/2 cup vegetable oil (or melted coconut oil)
- 2 large eggs
- 1/2 cup milk (or buttermilk)
- 1 teaspoon baking powder
- 1/2 teaspoon baking soda
- 1/2 teaspoon salt
- 1 1/2 teaspoons ground cinnamon
- 1/2 teaspoon ground nutmeg
- 1/4 teaspoon ground ginger
- 1/4 teaspoon ground cloves
- 1/2 cup chopped nuts (such as walnuts or pecans, optional)
- 1/4 cup mini chocolate chips (optional, for added sweetness)

For the Topping (Optional):

- 2 tablespoons granulated sugar
- 1/2 teaspoon ground cinnamon

Instructions:

1. **Preheat the Oven:**
   - Preheat your oven to 350°F (175°C). Line a muffin tin with paper liners or lightly grease the cups.
2. **Prepare the Dry Ingredients:**
   - In a medium bowl, whisk together the flour, baking powder, baking soda, salt, ground cinnamon, nutmeg, ginger, and cloves.
3. **Mix the Wet Ingredients:**
   - In a large bowl, combine the pumpkin puree, granulated sugar, brown sugar, oil, eggs, and milk. Mix well until smooth.
4. **Combine Wet and Dry Ingredients:**
   - Gradually add the dry ingredients to the wet ingredients, mixing just until combined. Be careful not to overmix.
   - Fold in the chopped nuts and mini chocolate chips, if using.
5. **Fill the Muffin Tin:**
   - Divide the batter evenly among the muffin cups, filling each about 2/3 full.
6. **Add Topping (Optional):**
   - In a small bowl, mix the granulated sugar with ground cinnamon.

- Sprinkle a little bit of this mixture on top of each muffin before baking for a sweet, spiced crunch.
7. **Bake the Muffins:**
   - Bake in the preheated oven for 18-22 minutes, or until a toothpick inserted into the center of a muffin comes out clean.
8. **Cool:**
   - Allow the muffins to cool in the pan for 5 minutes, then transfer them to a wire rack to cool completely.

Tips:

- **Pumpkin Puree:** Make sure to use pure pumpkin puree, not pumpkin pie filling which contains added spices and sugar.
- **Storage:** Store muffins in an airtight container at room temperature for up to 3 days, or freeze for longer storage.
- **Flavor Variations:** Add a handful of dried cranberries or raisins for extra sweetness and texture.

Fall Pumpkin Spice Muffins are a delicious way to enjoy the cozy flavors of autumn. They're perfect for enjoying with a cup of coffee or tea, or simply as a delightful treat throughout the season. Enjoy!

Winter Baked Ziti

Ingredients:

- **1 lb ziti pasta**
- **1 lb ground beef** (or Italian sausage, or a mix of both)
- **1 onion** (chopped)
- **3 cloves garlic** (minced)
- **1 (28 oz) can crushed tomatoes**
- **1 (14.5 oz) can diced tomatoes**
- **2 tablespoons tomato paste**
- **1 teaspoon dried basil**
- **1 teaspoon dried oregano**
- **1/2 teaspoon red pepper flakes** (optional, for heat)
- **Salt and black pepper** (to taste)
- **1/2 cup grated Parmesan cheese**
- **2 cups shredded mozzarella cheese**
- **1/2 cup chopped fresh parsley** (optional, for garnish)

Instructions:

1. **Preheat the Oven:**
   - Preheat your oven to 375°F (190°C). Lightly grease a large baking dish (about 9x13 inches).
2. **Cook the Pasta:**
   - Bring a large pot of salted water to a boil. Cook the ziti according to the package instructions until al dente. Drain and set aside.
3. **Prepare the Meat Sauce:**
   - In a large skillet or saucepan, cook the ground beef (or sausage) over medium heat until browned and cooked through. Break up the meat into crumbles as it cooks. Drain any excess fat.
   - Add the chopped onion and cook until softened, about 5 minutes.
   - Stir in the minced garlic and cook for 1 minute until fragrant.
   - Add the crushed tomatoes, diced tomatoes, and tomato paste. Stir to combine.
   - Season with dried basil, oregano, red pepper flakes (if using), salt, and black pepper. Simmer for 10-15 minutes to allow the flavors to meld.
4. **Combine Pasta and Sauce:**
   - In a large mixing bowl, combine the cooked ziti with the meat sauce. Stir until the pasta is evenly coated with the sauce.
5. **Assemble the Baked Ziti:**
   - Pour half of the pasta and sauce mixture into the prepared baking dish.
   - Sprinkle with 1/2 cup of mozzarella cheese.
   - Top with the remaining pasta and sauce mixture.
   - Sprinkle the remaining 1 1/2 cups of mozzarella cheese and the grated Parmesan cheese on top.

6. **Bake:**
   - Cover the baking dish with aluminum foil and bake in the preheated oven for 25 minutes.
   - Remove the foil and bake for an additional 10-15 minutes, or until the cheese is melted and bubbly and the top is golden brown.
7. **Garnish and Serve:**
   - Let the baked ziti cool for a few minutes before serving.
   - Garnish with chopped fresh parsley if desired.

Tips:

- **Make-Ahead:** Baked ziti can be assembled a day in advance and stored in the refrigerator until ready to bake. Just add a few extra minutes to the baking time if baking from cold.
- **Vegetarian Option:** Omit the meat and add extra vegetables like mushrooms, bell peppers, and spinach for a vegetarian version.
- **Cheese:** Feel free to use different cheeses or add ricotta cheese for a creamy layer in the middle.

Winter Baked Ziti is a comforting and satisfying dish that's perfect for cozy dinners or feeding a crowd. It's rich, cheesy, and full of flavor, making it a family favorite for the winter season. Enjoy!

Spring Green Goddess Quinoa Bowl

Ingredients:

- **1 cup quinoa** (uncooked)
- **2 cups water** (or vegetable broth for added flavor)
- **1 tablespoon olive oil**
- **1 cup snap peas** (trimmed and halved)
- **1 cup baby spinach**
- **1 cup cherry tomatoes** (halved)
- **1 cucumber** (diced)
- **1 avocado** (sliced)
- **1/4 cup thinly sliced radishes**
- **1/4 cup chopped fresh herbs** (such as parsley, chives, or basil)
- **Salt and black pepper** (to taste)

For the Green Goddess Dressing:

- **1/2 cup Greek yogurt**
- **1/4 cup fresh basil** (chopped)
- **1/4 cup fresh parsley** (chopped)
- **2 tablespoons lemon juice**
- **1 tablespoon olive oil**
- **1 clove garlic** (minced)
- **1 tablespoon Dijon mustard**
- **Salt and black pepper** (to taste)

Instructions:

1. **Cook the Quinoa:**
   - Rinse the quinoa under cold water.
   - In a medium saucepan, bring 2 cups of water (or vegetable broth) to a boil.
   - Add the quinoa, reduce heat to low, cover, and simmer for about 15 minutes, or until the quinoa is cooked and the liquid is absorbed.
   - Remove from heat and let it sit, covered, for 5 minutes. Fluff with a fork and let cool slightly.
2. **Prepare the Vegetables:**
   - While the quinoa is cooking, heat the olive oil in a small skillet over medium heat.
   - Add the snap peas and cook for 2-3 minutes until tender-crisp. Season with a pinch of salt and pepper.
   - Set aside.
3. **Make the Green Goddess Dressing:**
   - In a food processor or blender, combine the Greek yogurt, basil, parsley, lemon juice, olive oil, garlic, Dijon mustard, salt, and pepper.
   - Blend until smooth. Adjust seasoning to taste.

4. **Assemble the Quinoa Bowl:**
    - Divide the cooked quinoa among serving bowls.
    - Top with snap peas, baby spinach, cherry tomatoes, cucumber, avocado slices, and radishes.
    - Drizzle with the Green Goddess dressing.
5. **Garnish and Serve:**
    - Sprinkle with chopped fresh herbs and additional salt and pepper if desired.
    - Serve immediately or chill until ready to eat.

Tips:

- **Customize:** Feel free to add other spring vegetables like asparagus or artichokes, or add protein like grilled chicken or tofu for extra sustenance.
- **Dressing:** The Green Goddess dressing can be made ahead of time and stored in the refrigerator for up to a week.
- **Quinoa:** For added flavor, consider cooking the quinoa in vegetable broth or adding some fresh herbs to the cooking water.

The Spring Green Goddess Quinoa Bowl is a nutritious and flavorful way to enjoy the fresh ingredients of spring. It's light, refreshing, and packed with vibrant colors and textures. Enjoy this healthy and delicious meal!

Summer Watermelon Feta Salad

Ingredients:

- **4 cups seedless watermelon** (cut into bite-sized cubes)
- **1 cup crumbled feta cheese**
- **1/4 cup fresh mint leaves** (chopped)
- **1/4 cup red onion** (thinly sliced)
- **1/4 cup cucumber** (diced, optional)
- **2 tablespoons extra-virgin olive oil**
- **1 tablespoon balsamic vinegar** (or red wine vinegar)
- **1 tablespoon honey** (optional, for a touch of sweetness)
- **Salt and black pepper** (to taste)
- **1/4 cup chopped walnuts** (optional, for added crunch)

Instructions:

1. **Prepare the Watermelon:**
   - Cut the watermelon into bite-sized cubes and place them in a large salad bowl.
2. **Add the Feta and Mint:**
   - Crumble the feta cheese over the watermelon.
   - Sprinkle the chopped mint leaves on top.
3. **Add Optional Ingredients:**
   - If using, add the thinly sliced red onion and diced cucumber for extra flavor and crunch.
4. **Make the Dressing:**
   - In a small bowl or jar, whisk together the olive oil, balsamic vinegar, and honey (if using). Season with a pinch of salt and black pepper.
5. **Assemble the Salad:**
   - Drizzle the dressing over the watermelon and feta mixture.
   - Gently toss the salad to combine all the ingredients, being careful not to break up the watermelon cubes too much.
6. **Add Crunch (Optional):**
   - If desired, sprinkle chopped walnuts on top of the salad for added texture and flavor.
7. **Serve:**
   - Serve immediately, or chill in the refrigerator for up to 30 minutes before serving to let the flavors meld.

Tips:

- **Watermelon:** Choose a seedless variety for the best results. If your watermelon has seeds, make sure to remove them before cutting.
- **Mint:** Fresh mint adds a burst of flavor. If you don't have fresh mint, you can use fresh basil as an alternative.

- **Feta Cheese:** Use high-quality feta cheese for the best flavor. You can also use reduced-fat feta if you prefer.

Summer Watermelon Feta Salad is a simple yet elegant dish that's perfect for picnics, barbecues, or any summer meal. Its combination of sweet, savory, and tangy flavors makes it a refreshing and satisfying choice. Enjoy!

Fall Sweet Potato and Black Bean Tacos

Ingredients:

- **1 large sweet potato** (peeled and cut into 1/2-inch cubes)
- **1 tablespoon olive oil**
- **1 teaspoon ground cumin**
- **1 teaspoon smoked paprika**
- **1/2 teaspoon chili powder**
- **1/2 teaspoon garlic powder**
- **Salt and black pepper** (to taste)
- **1 can (15 oz) black beans** (rinsed and drained)
- **1/2 cup corn kernels** (fresh, frozen, or canned)
- **1/2 cup red onion** (diced)
- **1/2 cup chopped fresh cilantro**
- **8 small corn or flour tortillas**
- **1 avocado** (sliced)
- **1 cup shredded lettuce** (optional)
- **1/2 cup crumbled feta cheese** (or cotija cheese, optional)
- **Lime wedges** (for serving)
- **Sour cream or Greek yogurt** (optional, for topping)
- **Hot sauce** (optional, for added heat)

Instructions:

1. **Roast the Sweet Potatoes:**
    - Preheat your oven to 400°F (200°C).
    - On a baking sheet, toss the sweet potato cubes with olive oil, ground cumin, smoked paprika, chili powder, garlic powder, salt, and black pepper.
    - Spread the sweet potatoes in a single layer and roast for 25-30 minutes, or until tender and slightly caramelized, stirring halfway through.
2. **Prepare the Black Beans and Corn:**
    - While the sweet potatoes are roasting, heat a small skillet over medium heat
    - Add the black beans and corn to the skillet. Cook, stirring occasionally, until heated through (about 5 minutes). Season with a pinch of salt and pepper.
3. **Prepare the Toppings:**
    - Dice the red onion, chop the cilantro, slice the avocado, and prepare any other desired toppings.
4. **Warm the Tortillas:**
    - Heat the tortillas in a dry skillet over medium heat for about 30 seconds on each side, or wrap them in foil and warm them in the oven for a few minutes.
5. **Assemble the Tacos:**
    - Spread a few spoonfuls of the roasted sweet potatoes in the center of each tortilla.
    - Top with the black beans and corn mixture.

- Add shredded lettuce (if using), diced red onion, chopped cilantro, and avocado slices.
- Sprinkle with crumbled feta or cotija cheese, if desired.
- Add a dollop of sour cream or Greek yogurt and a splash of hot sauce, if using.

6. **Serve:**
   - Serve the tacos with lime wedges on the side for squeezing over the top.

Tips:

- **Sweet Potatoes:** Make sure to cut the sweet potato cubes into uniform sizes for even roasting.
- **Beans:** For added flavor, you can season the black beans with a bit of cumin and paprika.
- **Toppings:** Feel free to customize with other favorite taco toppings like salsa or pickled jalapeños.

Fall Sweet Potato and Black Bean Tacos offer a wonderful combination of sweet, savory, and spicy flavors that highlight the best of autumn produce. They're perfect for a cozy dinner or casual get-together. Enjoy these flavorful and satisfying tacos!

Winter Chicken Pot Pie

Ingredients:

- **1 lb boneless, skinless chicken breasts or thighs** (cut into bite-sized pieces)
- **2 tablespoons olive oil**
- **1 medium onion** (diced)
- **2 cloves garlic** (minced)
- **1 cup carrots** (diced)
- **1 cup celery** (diced)
- **1 cup frozen peas** (or fresh if preferred)
- **1 cup frozen corn** (or fresh if preferred)
- **1/3 cup all-purpose flour**
- **2 cups chicken broth**
- **1 cup milk** (whole or 2%)
- **1 teaspoon dried thyme**
- **1 teaspoon dried rosemary**
- **Salt and black pepper** (to taste)
- **1/2 cup heavy cream** (optional, for extra creaminess)
- **1 tablespoon chopped fresh parsley** (optional, for garnish)
- **1 prepared pie crust** (store-bought or homemade, for top and bottom)
- **1 egg** (beaten, for egg wash)

Instructions:

1. **Preheat the Oven:**
   - Preheat your oven to 425°F (220°C).
2. **Cook the Chicken:**
   - In a large skillet or Dutch oven, heat the olive oil over medium heat.
   - Add the chicken pieces and cook until they are no longer pink in the center, about 5-7 minutes. Remove the chicken from the skillet and set aside.
3. **Prepare the Vegetables:**
   - In the same skillet, add a little more olive oil if needed and sauté the onion, garlic, carrots, and celery until they are tender, about 5-7 minutes.
4. **Make the Sauce:**
   - Stir in the flour and cook for 1-2 minutes to remove the raw flour taste.
   - Gradually whisk in the chicken broth and milk. Continue to whisk until the mixture is smooth and starts to thicken, about 5 minutes.
   - Stir in the cooked chicken, peas, and corn. Season with dried thyme, rosemary, salt, and black pepper.
   - For extra creaminess, stir in the heavy cream (if using).
5. **Assemble the Pot Pie:**
   - Transfer the chicken and vegetable mixture into a prepared pie dish.
   - Place the pie crust over the filling. Trim any excess crust and crimp the edges to seal. Cut a few slits in the top crust to allow steam to escape.

- Brush the top crust with the beaten egg for a golden finish.
6. **Bake:**
    - Bake in the preheated oven for 30-35 minutes, or until the crust is golden brown and the filling is bubbly.
    - If the edges of the crust start to brown too quickly, cover them with aluminum foil.
7. **Cool and Serve:**
    - Allow the pot pie to cool for 5-10 minutes before serving. This will help the filling set and make it easier to slice.

Tips:

- **Pie Crust:** You can use store-bought pie crusts or make your own. If using a frozen crust, thaw it according to the package instructions.
- **Vegetables:** Feel free to customize with other vegetables like mushrooms, green beans, or potatoes.
- **Make-Ahead:** The filling can be prepared in advance and stored in the refrigerator for up to 2 days. Assemble and bake when ready to serve.

Winter Chicken Pot Pie is the ultimate comfort food for chilly days, offering a warm and satisfying meal that's sure to please the whole family. Enjoy!

Spring Radish and Cucumber Salad

Ingredients:

- **1 bunch radishes** (about 8-10 radishes, trimmed and thinly sliced)
- **1 large cucumber** (peeled if desired, sliced thinly)
- **1/4 small red onion** (thinly sliced, optional)
- **1/4 cup fresh dill** (chopped, or substitute with parsley or mint)
- **2 tablespoons extra-virgin olive oil**
- **1 tablespoon white wine vinegar** (or apple cider vinegar)
- **1 teaspoon Dijon mustard**
- **1 teaspoon honey** (or maple syrup, optional for sweetness)
- **Salt and black pepper** (to taste)
- **1 tablespoon capers** (optional, for added brininess)
- **1/4 cup crumbled feta cheese** (optional, for added creaminess)

Instructions:

1. **Prepare the Vegetables:**
   - Thinly slice the radishes and cucumber. If using, thinly slice the red onion.
   - Place the radishes, cucumber, and red onion (if using) in a large bowl.
2. **Make the Dressing:**
   - In a small bowl or jar, whisk together the olive oil, white wine vinegar, Dijon mustard, and honey (if using). Season with salt and black pepper to taste.
3. **Combine and Toss:**
   - Pour the dressing over the sliced radishes, cucumber, and red onion.
   - Toss gently to combine, ensuring that the vegetables are evenly coated with the dressing.
4. **Add Herbs and Optional Ingredients:**
   - Stir in the chopped fresh dill.
   - If using, add capers and crumbled feta cheese to the salad. Gently toss again to distribute.
5. **Serve:**
   - Serve the salad immediately, or chill it in the refrigerator for about 30 minutes to let the flavors meld.

Tips:

- **Radishes:** For a milder flavor, you can soak the sliced radishes in cold water for about 10 minutes before using.
- **Cucumber:** If the cucumber has a thick skin, peeling it can make the salad more tender and less bitter.
- **Herbs:** Fresh herbs can be swapped based on your preference or availability. Mint or parsley also work well.

- **Make-Ahead:** The salad can be prepared a few hours in advance. Just be sure to add the fresh herbs and optional ingredients just before serving to keep them fresh.

Spring Radish and Cucumber Salad is a light, crunchy, and flavorful dish that brings a taste of spring to your table. It's perfect for picnics, barbecues, or as a fresh side for any meal. Enjoy this vibrant and easy-to-make salad!

Summer BBQ Pulled Pork Sandwiches

Ingredients:

For the Pulled Pork:

- **3-4 lbs pork shoulder** (also called pork butt)
- **1 tablespoon paprika**
- **1 tablespoon brown sugar**
- **1 teaspoon garlic powder**
- **1 teaspoon onion powder**
- **1 teaspoon ground cumin**
- **1 teaspoon salt**
- **1/2 teaspoon black pepper**
- **1/2 teaspoon cayenne pepper** (optional, for heat)
- **1 cup BBQ sauce** (store-bought or homemade)
- **1 cup chicken broth** (or water)
- **1 tablespoon apple cider vinegar**

For Serving:

- **8 soft hamburger buns** (or your favorite type of bread)
- **Coleslaw** (optional, for topping)
- **Pickles** (optional, for topping)

Instructions:

1. **Prepare the Pork:**
   - In a small bowl, mix together the paprika, brown sugar, garlic powder, onion powder, ground cumin, salt, black pepper, and cayenne pepper (if using).
   - Rub the spice mixture all over the pork shoulder.
2. **Cook the Pork:**
   - **Slow Cooker Method:**
     - Place the seasoned pork shoulder in a slow cooker.
     - Pour the chicken broth and apple cider vinegar over the pork.
     - Cover and cook on low for 8-10 hours, or until the pork is very tender and easily shreds with a fork.
   - **Oven Method:**
     - Preheat your oven to 300°F (150°C).
     - Place the seasoned pork shoulder in a large Dutch oven or oven-safe pot.
     - Pour the chicken broth and apple cider vinegar over the pork.
     - Cover and roast for 4-5 hours, or until the pork is tender and easily shreds with a fork.
3. **Shred the Pork:**

- Once the pork is cooked, remove it from the slow cooker or pot and transfer it to a cutting board.
- Use two forks to shred the pork into bite-sized pieces.
- Return the shredded pork to the cooking juices in the slow cooker or pot.

4. **Add BBQ Sauce:**
   - Stir in the BBQ sauce, making sure the pork is well-coated.
   - Continue to cook for an additional 30 minutes on low (if using a slow cooker) or heat on the stove until warmed through (if using the oven method).

5. **Assemble the Sandwiches:**
   - Toast the hamburger buns if desired.
   - Spoon the BBQ pulled pork onto the bottom half of each bun.
   - Top with coleslaw and pickles if using.
   - Place the top half of the bun on top and serve.

Tips:

- **Coleslaw:** A tangy coleslaw adds a nice crunch and balances the richness of the pulled pork. You can use store-bought coleslaw or make your own.
- **BBQ Sauce:** Choose your favorite BBQ sauce, or make your own for a personalized touch.
- **Make-Ahead:** The pulled pork can be made a day in advance and stored in the refrigerator. Reheat before serving.

Summer BBQ Pulled Pork Sandwiches are perfect for picnics, backyard barbecues, or any casual get-together. The combination of tender, flavorful pork and the tangy BBQ sauce makes for a delicious and satisfying meal. Enjoy!

Fall Maple Glazed Brussels Sprouts

Ingredients:

- **1 1/2 lbs Brussels sprouts** (trimmed and halved)
- **2 tablespoons olive oil**
- **1/4 cup pure maple syrup**
- **2 tablespoons balsamic vinegar**
- **1 tablespoon Dijon mustard**
- **1/2 teaspoon garlic powder**
- **Salt and black pepper** (to taste)
- **1/4 cup chopped pecans** (optional, for added crunch)
- **1/4 cup dried cranberries** (optional, for a touch of sweetness)

Instructions:

1. **Preheat the Oven:**
    - Preheat your oven to 400°F (200°C).
2. **Prepare the Brussels Sprouts:**
    - Trim the ends off the Brussels sprouts and cut them in half.
    - In a large bowl, toss the halved Brussels sprouts with olive oil, salt, and black pepper until well coated.
3. **Roast the Brussels Sprouts:**
    - Spread the Brussels sprouts in a single layer on a baking sheet.
    - Roast in the preheated oven for 20-25 minutes, or until they are golden brown and tender, stirring halfway through for even roasting.
4. **Make the Maple Glaze:**
    - While the Brussels sprouts are roasting, in a small saucepan, combine the maple syrup, balsamic vinegar, Dijon mustard, and garlic powder.
    - Bring to a simmer over medium heat, stirring occasionally. Let it cook for about 5 minutes, or until the glaze has thickened slightly. Remove from heat.
5. **Combine and Serve:**
    - Once the Brussels sprouts are roasted, transfer them to a large bowl.
    - Drizzle the maple glaze over the roasted Brussels sprouts and toss to coat evenly.
    - If using, sprinkle with chopped pecans and dried cranberries for added texture and flavor.
6. **Serve:**
    - Serve immediately while still warm.

Tips:

- **Roasting:** For best results, make sure the Brussels sprouts are spread out in a single layer on the baking sheet. This helps them roast evenly and get a nice caramelized exterior.

- **Maple Syrup:** Use pure maple syrup for the best flavor. Avoid pancake syrup, as it often contains artificial ingredients.
- **Pecans and Cranberries:** These are optional but add a lovely contrast of textures and a touch of sweetness to the dish.

Fall Maple Glazed Brussels Sprouts make a wonderful side dish for holiday meals, weeknight dinners, or any occasion where you want to enjoy a seasonal, flavorful vegetable. Enjoy the perfect balance of sweet and savory in every bite!

Winter Creamy Tomato Soup

Ingredients:

- **2 tablespoons olive oil**
- **1 medium onion** (diced)
- **2 cloves garlic** (minced)
- **2 cans (14.5 oz each) diced tomatoes** (with their juice)
- **1 cup tomato sauce**
- **2 cups chicken broth** (or vegetable broth)
- **1 teaspoon dried basil**
- **1 teaspoon dried oregano**
- **1/2 teaspoon sugar** (optional, to balance acidity)
- **Salt and black pepper** (to taste)
- **1/2 cup heavy cream** (or whole milk)
- **Fresh basil** (chopped, for garnish)
- **Grated Parmesan cheese** (optional, for garnish)
- **Croutons or crusty bread** (optional, for serving)

Instructions:

1. **Sauté Aromatics:**
   - Heat olive oil in a large pot over medium heat.
   - Add the onion and cook until translucent, about 5 minutes.
   - Stir in garlic and cook for another 1-2 minutes until fragrant.
2. **Add Tomatoes:**
   - Pour in diced tomatoes, tomato sauce, and chicken broth.
   - Stir in basil, oregano, and sugar (if using). Season with salt and pepper.
3. **Simmer:**
   - Bring to a boil, then reduce heat and simmer for 20 minutes.
4. **Blend Soup:**
   - Use an immersion blender to puree the soup until smooth. Alternatively, carefully blend in batches using a countertop blender.
5. **Add Cream:**
   - Stir in the heavy cream and heat through, but avoid boiling.
6. **Serve:**
   - Ladle into bowls, garnish with fresh basil and Parmesan cheese if desired.
   - Serve with croutons or crusty bread.

Tips:

- **For Extra Smoothness:** Strain the soup through a fine mesh sieve after blending for an ultra-smooth texture.
- **Flavor Adjustments:** Adjust seasoning as needed and add more herbs or a dash of red pepper flakes for extra flavor.

This creamy tomato soup pairs wonderfully with a grilled cheese sandwich or a fresh green salad, making it a perfect choice for a comforting winter meal. Enjoy!

Spring Lemon Garlic Shrimp

Ingredients:

- **1 lb large shrimp** (peeled and deveined)
- **2 tablespoons olive oil**
- **4 cloves garlic** (minced)
- **1 lemon** (zested and juiced)
- **1/4 cup white wine** (optional, can substitute with chicken broth)
- **1/4 teaspoon red pepper flakes** (optional, for a bit of heat)
- **Salt and black pepper** (to taste)
- **2 tablespoons fresh parsley** (chopped, for garnish)
- **Lemon wedges** (for serving)
- **Cooked rice or pasta** (for serving, optional)

Instructions:

1. **Prepare the Shrimp:**
    - Pat the shrimp dry with paper towels and season them with salt and black pepper.
2. **Cook the Garlic:**
    - Heat olive oil in a large skillet over medium heat.
    - Add the minced garlic and cook for 1-2 minutes, until fragrant but not browned.
3. **Cook the Shrimp:**
    - Increase the heat to medium-high and add the shrimp to the skillet.
    - Cook the shrimp for 2-3 minutes on each side, or until they are pink and opaque
4. **Add Lemon and Wine:**
    - Stir in the lemon zest, lemon juice, and white wine (or chicken broth).
    - Cook for another 2 minutes, allowing the sauce to reduce slightly and the flavors to meld.
    - If using, add red pepper flakes at this stage for a bit of heat.
5. **Finish and Serve:**
    - Remove from heat and stir in the fresh parsley.
    - Serve immediately with lemon wedges on the side.
6. **Optional:**
    - For a complete meal, serve the lemon garlic shrimp over cooked rice or pasta.

Tips:

- **Shrimp Size:** Use large or jumbo shrimp for the best results, as they hold up well during cooking and offer a satisfying bite.
- **Wine Substitution:** If you prefer not to use wine, chicken broth or vegetable broth is a good substitute.
- **Extra Flavor:** For additional depth, you can add a splash of white wine vinegar or a sprinkle of Parmesan cheese just before serving.

Spring Lemon Garlic Shrimp is a vibrant and delicious dish that pairs well with a variety of sides. It's quick to prepare and packed with fresh flavors, making it a fantastic choice for a light and satisfying meal. Enjoy!

Summer Gazpacho

Ingredients:

- **6 ripe tomatoes** (core removed)
- **1 cucumber** (peeled and diced)
- **1 red bell pepper** (seeded and diced)
- **1 green bell pepper** (seeded and diced)
- **1 small red onion** (diced)
- **3 cloves garlic** (minced)
- **1/4 cup extra virgin olive oil**
- **2 tablespoons red wine vinegar** (or sherry vinegar)
- **1 teaspoon smoked paprika**
- **Salt and black pepper** (to taste)
- **1 cup tomato juice** (or vegetable broth)
- **Fresh basil or parsley** (chopped, for garnish)
- **Croutons** (optional, for garnish)

Instructions:

1. **Prepare the Vegetables:**
    - Roughly chop the tomatoes, cucumber, red bell pepper, green bell pepper, and red onion.
2. **Blend the Ingredients:**
    - In a blender or food processor, combine the chopped tomatoes, cucumber, bell peppers, red onion, and garlic.
    - Blend until smooth. If necessary, blend in batches.
3. **Season the Soup:**
    - Add the olive oil, red wine vinegar, smoked paprika, salt, and black pepper to the blended mixture.
    - Blend again to combine all the ingredients thoroughly.
4. **Adjust Consistency:**
    - If the soup is too thick, add tomato juice or vegetable broth to reach your desired consistency.
    - Blend again if necessary to incorporate the added liquid.
5. **Chill:**
    - Transfer the gazpacho to a large bowl or pitcher.
    - Cover and refrigerate for at least 2 hours, or until well chilled. This allows the flavors to meld together.
6. **Serve:**
    - Stir the gazpacho before serving.
    - Ladle into bowls and garnish with fresh basil or parsley and croutons if desired.

Tips:

- **Tomatoes:** Use the ripest tomatoes you can find for the best flavor.
- **Texture:** For a chunkier texture, pulse the ingredients in the blender instead of blending completely smooth.
- **Flavor Boost:** Adjust the seasoning to taste, adding more vinegar or a pinch of sugar if needed to balance the flavors.

Summer Gazpacho is a delightful and cooling dish that makes the most of seasonal vegetables. It's nutritious, refreshing, and an excellent way to enjoy the bounty of summer produce. Enjoy this light and tasty soup!

Fall Roasted Apple and Butternut Squash Salad

Ingredients:

- **1 small butternut squash** (peeled, seeded, and cubed)
- **2 apples** (cored and chopped)
- **2 tablespoons olive oil**
- **Salt and black pepper** (to taste)
- **1 teaspoon ground cinnamon** (optional)
- **4 cups mixed greens** (such as spinach, arugula, or baby kale)
- **1/4 cup dried cranberries**
- **1/4 cup pecans** (toasted, for added crunch)
- **1/4 cup crumbled feta cheese** (or goat cheese)
- **1/4 cup balsamic vinaigrette** (store-bought or homemade)

Instructions:

1. **Preheat the Oven:**
    - Preheat your oven to 400°F (200°C).
2. **Prepare the Vegetables and Apples:**
    - In a large bowl, toss the cubed butternut squash and chopped apples with olive oil, salt, black pepper, and cinnamon (if using).
3. **Roast:**
    - Spread the butternut squash and apples in a single layer on a baking sheet.
    - Roast in the preheated oven for 25-30 minutes, or until the squash is tender and caramelized and the apples are slightly softened. Stir halfway through for even roasting.
4. **Assemble the Salad:**
    - In a large salad bowl, combine the mixed greens, dried cranberries, toasted pecans, and crumbled feta cheese.
5. **Add Roasted Ingredients:**
    - Once the roasted squash and apples have cooled slightly, add them to the salad bowl.
6. **Dress and Serve:**
    - Drizzle with balsamic vinaigrette and toss gently to coat all ingredients evenly.
    - Serve immediately or refrigerate until ready to serve.

Tips:

- **Toasting Pecans:** Toasting pecans enhances their flavor. Simply heat them in a dry skillet over medium heat for 3-5 minutes, shaking the pan occasionally, until fragrant.
- **Vinaigrette:** You can make your own balsamic vinaigrette by whisking together balsamic vinegar, olive oil, a touch of honey, and Dijon mustard.
- **Texture Variation:** For extra crunch, consider adding some roasted pumpkin seeds or crispy chickpeas.

This Fall Roasted Apple and Butternut Squash Salad is a deliciously seasonal dish that combines sweet and savory flavors with a variety of textures. It's perfect for autumn gatherings and makes a satisfying addition to any meal. Enjoy!

Winter Sausage and Kale Soup

Ingredients:

- 1 tablespoon olive oil
- 1 pound Italian sausage (bulk, not in casings)
- 1 medium onion (diced)
- 2 cloves garlic (minced)
- 3 medium carrots (peeled and sliced)
- 3 celery stalks (sliced)
- 4 cups low-sodium chicken broth
- 2 cups water
- 1 large potato (diced, such as Yukon Gold or Russet)
- 1 teaspoon dried thyme
- 1 teaspoon dried rosemary
- 1 bay leaf
- 2 cups chopped kale (stems removed)
- Salt and black pepper (to taste)
- 1/2 cup grated Parmesan cheese (optional, for garnish)

Instructions:

1. **Cook the Sausage:**
    - In a large pot or Dutch oven, heat olive oil over medium heat.
    - Add the sausage and cook, breaking it up with a spoon, until browned and cooked through. Remove sausage with a slotted spoon and set aside.
2. **Sauté Vegetables:**
    - In the same pot, add the diced onion and cook until translucent, about 5 minutes.
    - Stir in the garlic and cook for an additional 1 minute until fragrant.
3. **Add Carrots and Celery:**
    - Add the carrots and celery to the pot, and cook for about 5 minutes until they start to soften.
4. **Simmer the Soup:**
    - Return the cooked sausage to the pot.
    - Pour in the chicken broth and water.
    - Add the diced potato, thyme, rosemary, and bay leaf.
    - Bring to a boil, then reduce heat and simmer for 20 minutes, or until the potatoes and vegetables are tender.
5. **Add Kale:**
    - Stir in the chopped kale and cook for an additional 5 minutes until the kale is wilted and tender.
6. **Season and Serve:**
    - Season the soup with salt and black pepper to taste.
    - Remove the bay leaf before serving.
7. **Optional:**

- Garnish with grated Parmesan cheese if desired.

Tips:

- **Sausage:** Use Italian sausage for extra flavor, or substitute with turkey sausage for a lighter option.
- **Kale:** Remove the tough stems from the kale before chopping it.
- **Storage:** This soup keeps well in the refrigerator for up to 4 days and can be frozen for up to 3 months.

Winter Sausage and Kale Soup is a warming, hearty meal that's perfect for cold days. It's rich in flavor and nutrients, making it an excellent choice for a cozy and satisfying dinner. Enjoy!

Spring Pea and Mint Pesto Pasta

Ingredients:

For the Pesto:

- 2 cups fresh peas (you can use frozen peas if fresh is not available)
- 1 cup fresh mint leaves
- 1/2 cup fresh basil leaves (optional, for added flavor)
- 1/4 cup pine nuts (or walnuts as a substitute)
- 1/4 cup grated Parmesan cheese
- 2-3 cloves garlic
- 1/4 cup extra-virgin olive oil
- Juice of 1 lemon
- Salt and pepper to taste

For the Pasta:

- 12 oz (340 g) pasta (like linguine, fettuccine, or your favorite type)
- 1 cup cherry tomatoes, halved (optional, for added freshness and color)
- Extra Parmesan for serving
- Additional mint leaves for garnish (optional)

Instructions:

1. **Cook the Pasta:**
    - Bring a large pot of salted water to a boil.
    - Cook the pasta according to the package instructions until al dente. Reserve 1/2 cup of pasta water before draining.
    - Drain the pasta and return it to the pot.
2. **Prepare the Pesto:**
    - If using fresh peas, blanch them in boiling water for 2-3 minutes, then transfer them to an ice bath to cool. Drain well.
    - In a food processor or blender, combine the peas, mint leaves, basil (if using), pine nuts, Parmesan cheese, and garlic. Pulse until finely chopped.
    - With the processor running, gradually add the olive oil and lemon juice. Blend until smooth. If the pesto is too thick, add a bit of the reserved pasta water to reach your desired consistency.
    - Season with salt and pepper to taste.
3. **Combine Pasta and Pesto:**
    - Toss the drained pasta with the pea and mint pesto until well coated. If needed, add some of the reserved pasta water to help mix everything together and achieve the desired consistency.
4. **Add Cherry Tomatoes (Optional):**

- If using, toss the cherry tomatoes into the pasta just before serving for a burst of freshness and color.
5. **Serve:**
    - Divide the pasta among plates. Garnish with extra Parmesan cheese and additional mint leaves if desired.

Enjoy your vibrant and fresh Spring Pea and Mint Pesto Pasta!

Summer Grilled Chicken Caesar Salad

Ingredients:

For the Salad:

- 2 boneless, skinless chicken breasts
- 1 tablespoon olive oil
- Salt and pepper, to taste
- 1 large head of Romaine lettuce, chopped
- 1/2 cup cherry tomatoes, halved
- 1/4 cup red onion, thinly sliced
- 1/4 cup grated Parmesan cheese
- Croutons (store-bought or homemade)

For the Dressing:

- 1/2 cup mayonnaise
- 2 tablespoons lemon juice
- 1 tablespoon Dijon mustard
- 2 cloves garlic, minced
- 1/4 cup grated Parmesan cheese
- Salt and pepper, to taste

Instructions:

1. **Grill the Chicken:**
    - Preheat your grill to medium-high heat.
    - Rub the chicken breasts with olive oil, salt, and pepper.
    - Grill the chicken for 6-8 minutes per side, or until fully cooked and juices run clear. Let it rest for a few minutes, then slice into strips.
2. **Prepare the Dressing:**
    - In a bowl, whisk together mayonnaise, lemon juice, Dijon mustard, minced garlic, Parmesan cheese, salt, and pepper. Adjust seasoning to taste.
3. **Assemble the Salad:**
    - In a large bowl, combine chopped Romaine lettuce cherry tomatoes, red onion and Parmesan cheese.
    - Add the grilled chicken on top.
    - Drizzle with Caesar dressing and toss gently to coat.
4. **Serve:**
    - Top with croutons and serve immediately.

Enjoy your refreshing Summer Grilled Chicken Caesar Salad!

Fall Spiced Apple Cider

Ingredients:

- 1 gallon apple cider
- 1 orange, sliced
- 6 whole cloves
- 3 cinnamon sticks
- 1 teaspoon whole allspice berries
- 1/2 teaspoon ground nutmeg
- 1-2 tablespoons maple syrup or honey (to taste)

Instructions:

1. **Combine Ingredients:**
   - In a large pot, combine apple cider, orange slices, cloves, cinnamon sticks, allspice berries, and nutmeg.
2. **Simmer:**
   - Bring to a boil, then reduce heat and simmer for about 20-30 minutes to let the spices infuse.
3. **Sweeten:**
   - Stir in maple syrup or honey to taste.
4. **Serve:**
   - Strain out the spices and serve hot.

Enjoy your warm, spiced apple cider!

Winter Beef Stroganoff

Ingredients:

- **For the Beef:**
    - 1 lb (450 g) beef sirloin or tenderloin, thinly sliced into strips
    - 2 tablespoons vegetable oil or butter
    - Salt and pepper, to taste
- **For the Sauce:**
    - 1 medium onion, finely chopped
    - 2 cloves garlic, minced
    - 8 oz (225 g) mushrooms, sliced
    - 1 tablespoon flour
    - 1 cup beef broth
    - 1 cup sour cream
    - 2 tablespoons Dijon mustard
    - 1 tablespoon Worcestershire sauce
    - 1 teaspoon paprika
    - 1/2 teaspoon dried thyme (optional)
    - 1 tablespoon chopped fresh parsley (for garnish)
- **For Serving:**
    - Cooked egg noodles, rice, or mashed potatoes

Instructions:

1. **Cook the Beef:**
    - Heat the vegetable oil or butter in a large skillet over medium-high heat.
    - Season the beef strips with salt and pepper.
    - Sear the beef in batches until browned on all sides but not fully cooked. Remove and set aside.
2. **Prepare the Sauce:**
    - In the same skillet, add a bit more oil or butter if needed. Add the chopped onion and cook until softened, about 5 minutes.
    - Add the garlic and sliced mushrooms. Cook until mushrooms are browned and tender, about 5-7 minutes.
    - Sprinkle the flour over the mushroom mixture and stir well to coat. Cook for another 1-2 minutes.
    - Gradually add the beef broth, stirring constantly to prevent lumps. Bring to a simmer and cook for 5 minutes, allowing the sauce to thicken slightly.
3. **Combine Ingredients:**
    - Reduce heat to low and stir in the sour cream, Dijon mustard, Worcestershire sauce, paprika, and dried thyme. Mix until well combined.
    - Return the browned beef strips to the skillet and simmer gently for 5-10 minutes, or until the beef is cooked through and the sauce is thickened to your liking.

4. **Serve:**
    - Serve the beef stroganoff over cooked egg noodles, rice, or mashed potatoes.
    - Garnish with chopped fresh parsley.

Enjoy your comforting and creamy Winter Beef Stroganoff!

Spring Roasted Beet Salad

Ingredients:

For the Salad:

- 4 medium beets, trimmed and scrubbed
- 2 tablespoons olive oil
- Salt and pepper, to taste
- 4 cups mixed greens (like arugula, spinach, or spring mix)
- 1/4 cup crumbled feta cheese or goat cheese
- 1/4 cup toasted walnuts or pecans
- 1/4 cup thinly sliced red onion (optional)
- 1/2 cup fresh herbs (like parsley or dill), chopped (optional)

For the Dressing:

- 3 tablespoons extra-virgin olive oil
- 1 tablespoon balsamic vinegar
- 1 tablespoon honey or maple syrup
- 1 teaspoon Dijon mustard
- Salt and pepper, to taste

Instructions:

1. **Roast the Beets:**
    - Preheat your oven to 400°F (200°C).
    - Rub the beets with olive oil and season with salt and pepper.
    - Wrap each beet in aluminum foil and place them on a baking sheet.
    - Roast for 45-60 minutes, or until a knife or fork easily pierces through the beets.
    - Let them cool slightly, then peel and cut into wedges or slices.
2. **Prepare the Dressing:**
    - In a small bowl, whisk together the olive oil, balsamic vinegar, honey or maple syrup, Dijon mustard, salt, and pepper.
3. **Assemble the Salad:**
    - In a large bowl, toss the mixed greens with a little of the dressing.
    - Arrange the roasted beet slices on top of the greens.
    - Sprinkle with crumbled feta or goat cheese, toasted nuts, and thinly sliced red onion if using.
    - Drizzle with more dressing and sprinkle with fresh herbs if desired.
4. **Serve:**
    - Serve immediately or chill for a bit before serving if you prefer a cooler salad.

Enjoy your refreshing and colorful Spring Roasted Beet Salad!

Summer Mango Salsa

Ingredients:

- 2 ripe mangos, peeled and diced
- 1 red bell pepper, finely diced
- 1/2 small red onion, finely chopped
- 1 jalapeño, seeded and minced (optional, for heat)
- 1/4 cup fresh cilantro, chopped
- Juice of 1 lime
- Salt and pepper, to taste

Instructions:

1. **Combine Ingredients:**
    - In a medium bowl, mix together the diced mango, red bell pepper, red onion, and jalapeño.
2. **Add Flavor:**
    - Stir in the chopped cilantro and lime juice.
3. **Season:**
    - Season with salt and pepper to taste.
4. **Chill:**
    - Let the salsa sit for about 15-30 minutes to let the flavors meld.

Serve with tortilla chips, grilled chicken, or fish for a vibrant summer dish!

Fall Pumpkin Ravioli

Ingredients:

- 1 cup pureed pumpkin (canned or fresh)
- 1/2 cup ricotta cheese
- 1/4 cup grated Parmesan cheese
- 1/4 teaspoon ground nutmeg
- 1/4 teaspoon ground cinnamon
- Salt and pepper, to taste

Instructions:

1. **Mix Filling:**
    - In a bowl, combine the pumpkin puree, ricotta cheese, Parmesan cheese, nutmeg, cinnamon, salt, and pepper. Mix until well combined. Set aside.

Ravioli Dough:

Ingredients:

- 2 cups all-purpose flour
- 3 large eggs
- 1/2 teaspoon salt
- 1 tablespoon olive oil

Instructions:

1. **Make Dough:**
    - In a large bowl, make a mound of flour and create a well in the center. Crack the eggs into the well, add the salt and olive oil.
    - Gradually mix the flour into the eggs until a dough forms. Knead on a lightly floured surface for about 8-10 minutes, until smooth and elastic. If the dough is too sticky, add a little more flour.
2. **Rest Dough:**
    - Wrap the dough in plastic wrap and let it rest for at least 30 minutes at room temperature.

Assembly:

Ingredients:

- Flour, for dusting
- 1 egg, beaten (for sealing the ravioli)

Instructions:

1. **Roll Out Dough:**
   - Divide the dough into two portions. Roll out each portion on a floured surface into thin sheets, about 1/16 inch thick.
2. **Form Ravioli:**
   - Place spoonfuls of filling (about 1 teaspoon each) spaced evenly on one sheet of dough.
   - Brush around the filling with beaten egg. Place the second sheet of dough over the top and press around each mound of filling to seal.
   - Use a knife or ravioli cutter to cut out individual ravioli. Press the edges with a fork to ensure they are well sealed.
3. **Cook Ravioli:**
   - Bring a large pot of salted water to a boil. Add the ravioli in batches and cook for about 3-4 minutes, or until they float to the surface and are tender. Remove with a slotted spoon and drain.

Sage Butter Sauce:

Ingredients:

- 4 tablespoons unsalted butter
- 8-10 fresh sage leaves
- 1/4 cup grated Parmesan cheese
- Salt and pepper, to taste

Instructions:

1. **Make Sauce:**
   - In a large skillet, melt the butter over medium heat. Add the sage leaves and cook until the butter is golden brown and the sage is crispy, about 2-3 minutes. Be careful not to burn the butter.
2. **Combine:**
   - Toss the cooked ravioli gently in the sage butter sauce. Add grated Parmesan cheese and season with salt and pepper.

Serve:

- Serve the ravioli with extra Parmesan cheese and a few additional crispy sage leaves for garnish.

Enjoy your delicious Fall Pumpkin Ravioli!

Winter Cozy Chili

Ingredients:

For the Chili:

- 1 lb (450 g) ground beef or ground turkey
- 1 tablespoon olive oil
- 1 medium onion, diced
- 3 cloves garlic, minced
- 1 red bell pepper, diced
- 1 green bell pepper, diced
- 2 medium carrots, diced
- 2 (15 oz) cans diced tomatoes
- 1 (15 oz) can tomato sauce
- 1 (15 oz) can kidney beans, drained and rinsed
- 1 (15 oz) can black beans, drained and rinsed
- 1 cup beef or chicken broth
- 2 tablespoons chili powder
- 1 tablespoon ground cumin
- 1 teaspoon paprika
- 1/2 teaspoon dried oregano
- 1/4 teaspoon cayenne pepper (optional, for heat)
- Salt and pepper, to taste

For Serving (optional):

- Shredded cheddar cheese
- Sour cream
- Chopped fresh cilantro
- Sliced green onions
- Crushed tortilla chips or cornbread

Instructions:

1. **Cook the Meat:**
   - In a large pot or Dutch oven, heat the olive oil over medium heat.
   - Add the ground beef or turkey and cook until browned, breaking it up with a spoon as it cooks. Drain excess fat if necessary.
2. **Sauté Vegetables:**
   - Add the diced onion, garlic, bell peppers, and carrots to the pot. Cook for about 5-7 minutes, or until the vegetables are softened.
3. **Add Spices:**
   - Stir in the chili powder, cumin, paprika, oregano, and cayenne pepper (if using). Cook for 1-2 minutes until fragrant.

4. **Combine Ingredients:**
   - Add the diced tomatoes, tomato sauce, kidney beans, black beans, and broth. Stir well to combine.
5. **Simmer:**
   - Bring the chili to a boil, then reduce heat to low and let it simmer uncovered for 30-45 minutes, stirring occasionally. The chili should thicken and the flavors will meld together.
6. **Season:**
   - Taste and adjust seasoning with salt and pepper as needed.
7. **Serve:**
   - Ladle the chili into bowls and top with shredded cheddar cheese, a dollop of sour cream, chopped cilantro, and sliced green onions if desired.
   - Serve with crushed tortilla chips or cornbread on the side.

Enjoy your hearty and warming Winter Cozy Chili!

Spring Avocado and Black Bean Tacos

Ingredients:

For the Tacos:

- 1 can (15 oz) black beans, drained and rinsed
- 1 tablespoon olive oil
- 1 teaspoon ground cumin
- 1/2 teaspoon smoked paprika
- 1/4 teaspoon garlic powder
- Salt and pepper, to taste
- 1 ripe avocado, diced
- 1 cup cherry tomatoes, halved
- 1/2 cup red onion, finely chopped
- 1/4 cup fresh cilantro, chopped
- 8 small corn or flour tortillas

For the Lime Crema (optional):

- 1/2 cup sour cream or Greek yogurt
- Juice of 1 lime
- 1 tablespoon chopped fresh cilantro
- Salt, to taste

Instructions:

1. **Prepare the Beans:**
    - In a skillet, heat olive oil over medium heat.
    - Add black beans, cumin, smoked paprika, garlic powder, salt, and pepper. Cook, stirring occasionally for about 5 minutes until the beans are heated through and well-seasoned.
2. **Make Lime Crema (optional):**
    - In a small bowl, mix sour cream or Greek yogurt with lime juice, chopped cilantro, and a pinch of salt. Adjust seasoning to taste.
3. **Assemble the Tacos:**
    - Warm the tortillas in a dry skillet or oven.
    - Spread a layer of seasoned black beans on each tortilla.
    - Top with diced avocado, cherry tomatoes, red onion, and cilantro.
4. **Add Lime Crema:**
    - Drizzle the lime crema over the tacos if using.
5. **Serve:**
    - Serve immediately with lime wedges on the side for extra zing.

Enjoy your vibrant and tasty Spring Avocado and Black Bean Tacos!

Summer Zucchini Noodles with Pesto

Ingredients:

For the Zucchini Noodles:

- 4 medium zucchinis, spiralized into noodles
- 1 tablespoon olive oil
- Salt and pepper, to taste

For the Pesto:

- 2 cups fresh basil leaves
- 1/2 cup pine nuts (or walnuts as a substitute)
- 1/2 cup grated Parmesan cheese
- 2-3 cloves garlic
- 1/4 cup extra-virgin olive oil
- Juice of 1 lemon
- Salt and pepper, to taste

Instructions:

1. **Prepare the Pesto:**
    - In a food processor or blender, combine basil, pine nuts, Parmesan cheese, and garlic. Pulse until finely chopped.
    - With the processor running, slowly add olive oil and lemon juice. Blend until smooth. Season with salt and pepper to taste.
2. **Cook the Zucchini Noodles:**
    - Heat olive oil in a large skillet over medium heat.
    - Add zucchini noodles and cook for 2-3 minutes, stirring gently, until just tender but still crisp. Season with salt and pepper.
3. **Combine:**
    - Toss the cooked zucchini noodles with the pesto until well coated.
4. **Serve:**
    - Serve immediately, optionally garnished with extra Parmesan cheese or fresh basil.

Enjoy your light and refreshing Summer Zucchini Noodles with Pesto!

Fall Pear and Gorgonzola Salad

Ingredients:

For the Salad:

- 4 cups mixed greens (like arugula, spinach, or baby kale)
- 2 ripe pears, cored and sliced
- 1/2 cup crumbled Gorgonzola cheese
- 1/4 cup toasted walnuts or pecans
- 1/4 red onion, thinly sliced (optional)
- 1/4 cup dried cranberries or pomegranate seeds (optional)

For the Dressing:

- 3 tablespoons extra-virgin olive oil
- 1 tablespoon balsamic vinegar
- 1 tablespoon honey or maple syrup
- 1 teaspoon Dijon mustard
- Salt and pepper, to taste

Instructions:

1. **Make the Dressing:**
   - In a small bowl, whisk together olive oil, balsamic vinegar, honey, Dijon mustard, salt, and pepper.
2. **Assemble the Salad:**
   - In a large bowl, toss the mixed greens with a bit of the dressing.
   - Top with sliced pears, crumbled Gorgonzola cheese, toasted nuts, and red onion if using.
   - Sprinkle with dried cranberries or pomegranate seeds if desired.
3. **Serve:**
   - Drizzle with more dressing and serve immediately.

Enjoy your flavorful and elegant Fall Pear and Gorgonzola Salad!

Winter Garlic Parmesan Roasted Potatoes

Ingredients:

- 1.5 lbs (680 g) baby potatoes or small Yukon Gold potatoes, halved or quartered
- 3 tablespoons olive oil
- 4 cloves garlic, minced
- 1/2 cup grated Parmesan cheese
- 1 teaspoon dried rosemary or thyme (optional)
- Salt and pepper, to taste
- Fresh parsley, chopped (for garnish)

Instructions:

1. **Preheat Oven:**
   - Preheat your oven to 425°F (220°C).
2. **Prepare Potatoes:**
   - In a large bowl, toss the potatoes with olive oil, minced garlic, Parmesan cheese, dried rosemary or thyme, salt, and pepper.
3. **Roast:**
   - Spread the potatoes in a single layer on a baking sheet.
   - Roast for 25-30 minutes, or until the potatoes are golden brown and crispy, stirring halfway through.
4. **Garnish:**
   - Remove from the oven and garnish with fresh parsley.

Serve hot and enjoy your delicious Winter Garlic Parmesan Roasted Potatoes!

Spring Carrot and Ginger Soup

Ingredients:

- 1.5 lbs (680 g) baby potatoes or small Yukon Gold potatoes, halved or quartered
- 3 tablespoons olive oil
- 4 cloves garlic, minced
- 1/2 cup grated Parmesan cheese
- 1 teaspoon dried rosemary or thyme (optional)
- Salt and pepper, to taste
- Fresh parsley, chopped (for garnish)

Instructions:

1. **Preheat Oven:**
    - Preheat your oven to 425°F (220°C).
2. **Prepare Potatoes:**
    - In a large bowl, toss the potatoes with olive oil, minced garlic, Parmesan cheese, dried rosemary or thyme, salt, and pepper.
3. **Roast:**
    - Spread the potatoes in a single layer on a baking sheet.
    - Roast for 25-30 minutes, or until the potatoes are golden brown and crispy, stirring halfway through.
4. **Garnish:**
    - Remove from the oven and garnish with fresh parsley.

Serve hot and enjoy your delicious Winter Garlic Parmesan Roasted Potatoes!

Spring Carrot and Ginger Soup

Ingredients:

- 1 tablespoon olive oil
- 1 medium onion, chopped
- 2 cloves garlic, minced
- 1 tablespoon fresh ginger, grated
- 6 cups carrots, peeled and chopped
- 4 cups vegetable or chicken broth
- 1 teaspoon ground cumin (optional)
- Salt and pepper, to taste
- 1/2 cup coconut milk or cream (optional, for creaminess)
- Fresh cilantro, chopped (for garnish)

Instructions:

1. **Sauté Aromatics:**
     - Heat olive oil in a large pot over medium heat. Add onion and cook until soft, about 5 minutes.
     - Add garlic and ginger; cook for another minute until fragrant.
2. **Cook Carrots:**
     - Add chopped carrots and cook for 5 minutes, stirring occasionally.
     - Pour in the broth and bring to a boil. Reduce heat and simmer until carrots are tender, about 20 minutes.
3. **Blend:**
     - Use an immersion blender to puree the soup until smooth. Alternatively, blend in batches using a countertop blender.
4. **Season and Serve:**
     - Stir in coconut milk or cream if using. Season with cumin, salt, and pepper.
     - Garnish with fresh cilantro before serving.

Enjoy your vibrant and soothing Spring Carrot and Ginger Soup!

Summer Lobster Rolls

Ingredients:

- 1 lb (450 g) cooked lobster meat, chopped
- 1/4 cup mayonnaise
- 1 tablespoon lemon juice
- 1 tablespoon fresh chives, chopped
- 1 tablespoon fresh dill or tarragon, chopped (optional)
- Salt and pepper, to taste
- 4 hot dog buns or split-top rolls
- 2 tablespoons unsalted butter
- Lettuce leaves (optional, for garnish)

Instructions:

1. **Prepare Lobster Filling:**
    - In a bowl, mix the lobster meat with mayonnaise, lemon juice, chives, dill or tarragon (if using), salt, and pepper. Adjust seasoning to taste.
2. **Toast Buns:**
    - Heat butter in a skillet over medium heat. Spread the remaining butter on the cut sides of the buns.
    - Toast the buns in the skillet until golden brown and crispy.
3. **Assemble Rolls:**
    - Place lettuce leaves on the bottom of each toasted bun if using.
    - Fill each bun generously with the lobster mixture.
4. **Serve:**
    - Serve immediately, garnished with extra chives or dill if desired.

Enjoy your fresh and tasty Summer Lobster Rolls!

Fall Cranberry Walnut Bread

Ingredients:

- 1 1/2 cups all-purpose flour
- 1/2 cup whole wheat flour
- 1/2 cup granulated sugar
- 1/2 cup brown sugar
- 1 teaspoon baking powder
- 1/2 teaspoon baking soda
- 1/4 teaspoon salt
- 1/2 teaspoon ground cinnamon
- 1/4 teaspoon ground nutmeg
- 1/2 cup unsalted butter, softened
- 2 large eggs
- 1 cup fresh or frozen cranberries, coarsely chopped
- 1/2 cup chopped walnuts
- 1/2 cup orange juice

Instructions:

1. **Preheat Oven:**
    - Preheat your oven to 350°F (175°C). Grease a 9x5-inch loaf pan.
2. **Mix Dry Ingredients:**
    - In a bowl, whisk together all-purpose flour, whole wheat flour, sugar, brown sugar, baking powder, baking soda, salt, cinnamon, and nutmeg.
3. **Cream Butter and Eggs:**
    - In a separate bowl, cream the softened butter with sugar until light and fluffy. Beat in the eggs one at a time.
4. **Combine Ingredients:**
    - Gradually mix in the dry ingredients alternately with orange juice until just combined. Fold in the chopped cranberries and walnuts.
5. **Bake:**
    - Pour the batter into the prepared loaf pan and smooth the top. Bake for 50-60 minutes, or until a toothpick inserted into the center comes out clean.
6. **Cool:**
    - Let the bread cool in the pan for 10 minutes, then transfer to a wire rack to cool completely before slicing.

Enjoy your fragrant and festive Fall Cranberry Walnut Bread!

Winter Creamy Mushroom Risotto

Ingredients:

- **For the Risotto:**
    - 1 cup Arborio rice
    - 4 cups chicken or vegetable broth
    - 1 cup dry white wine (optional, can substitute with extra broth)
    - 2 tablespoons olive oil
    - 1 medium onion, finely chopped
    - 2 cloves garlic, minced
    - 2 cups mushrooms (such as cremini, shiitake, or a mix), sliced
    - 1/2 cup grated Parmesan cheese
    - 2 tablespoons unsalted butter
    - Salt and pepper, to taste
    - Fresh parsley, chopped (for garnish)

Instructions:

1. **Prepare the Broth:**
    - In a saucepan, keep the broth warm over low heat.
2. **Sauté Mushrooms:**
    - In a large skillet or saucepan, heat olive oil over medium heat.
    - Add the sliced mushrooms and cook until they release their moisture and become golden brown, about 5-7 minutes. Remove from the pan and set aside.
3. **Cook the Aromatics:**
    - In the same skillet, add a bit more olive oil if needed and sauté the onion until translucent, about 5 minutes.
    - Add the garlic and cook for another minute until fragrant.
4. **Cook the Rice:**
    - Add the Arborio rice to the onion and garlic mixture. Stir for 1-2 minutes until the rice is lightly toasted and coated with oil.
    - Pour in the white wine (if using) and cook, stirring constantly, until the wine is mostly absorbed.
5. **Add Broth:**
    - Begin adding the warm broth to the rice one ladleful at a time, stirring frequently. Allow each addition to be absorbed before adding more. This process should take about 18-20 minutes. The rice should be creamy and just tender.
6. **Finish the Risotto:**
    - Once the rice is cooked, stir in the sautéed mushrooms.
    - Add the butter and Parmesan cheese, stirring until melted and well combined.
    - Season with salt and pepper to taste.
7. **Serve:**
    - Garnish with chopped fresh parsley and additional Parmesan cheese if desired.

Enjoy your rich and creamy Winter Mushroom Risotto!

Spring Artichoke and Lemon Pasta

Ingredients:

- 12 oz (340 g) pasta (such as penne or spaghetti)
- 1 tablespoon olive oil
- 1 small onion, finely chopped
- 2 cloves garlic, minced
- 1 can (14 oz) artichoke hearts, drained and quartered
- 1/2 cup white wine or vegetable broth
- Zest and juice of 1 lemon
- 1/4 cup grated Parmesan cheese
- 2 tablespoons fresh basil or parsley, chopped
- Salt and pepper, to taste

Instructions:

1. **Cook Pasta:**
   - Cook the pasta according to package instructions until al dente. Drain, reserving 1/2 cup of pasta water.
2. **Sauté Aromatics:**
   - In a large skillet, heat olive oil over medium heat.
   - Add the onion and cook until translucent, about 5 minutes.
   - Add the garlic and cook for another minute.
3. **Add Artichokes:**
   - Stir in the artichoke hearts and cook for 2-3 minutes.
4. **Deglaze and Flavor:**
   - Pour in the white wine or vegetable broth and cook until slightly reduced, about 2 minutes.
   - Stir in the lemon zest and juice.
5. **Combine Pasta:**
   - Add the cooked pasta to the skillet. Toss to combine, adding reserved pasta water a little at a time if needed to help coat the pasta.
6. **Finish:**
   - Stir in the Parmesan cheese and fresh basil or parsley. Season with salt and pepper to taste.
7. **Serve:**
   - Serve immediately, garnished with extra Parmesan cheese and herbs if desired.

Enjoy your bright and flavorful Spring Artichoke and Lemon Pasta!

Summer Grilled Vegetable Platter

Ingredients:

- **Vegetables:**
    - 1 large zucchini, sliced into rounds
    - 1 red bell pepper, cut into strips
    - 1 yellow bell pepper, cut into strips
    - 1 medium red onion, sliced into rounds
    - 8 oz (225 g) cherry tomatoes
    - 1 cup mushrooms, whole or halved
    - 1 cup asparagus spears (trimmed)
- **For Marinade:**
    - 1/4 cup olive oil
    - 2 tablespoons balsamic vinegar
    - 2 cloves garlic, minced
    - 1 teaspoon dried oregano
    - 1 teaspoon dried basil
    - Salt and pepper, to taste
- **For Serving:**
    - Fresh basil or parsley, chopped (optional)
    - Lemon wedges (optional)

Instructions:

1. **Prepare Marinade:**
    - In a small bowl, whisk together olive oil, balsamic vinegar, garlic, oregano, basil, salt, and pepper.
2. **Marinate Vegetables:**
    - Place vegetables in a large bowl or resealable plastic bag. Pour marinade over the vegetables and toss to coat. Let marinate for at least 30 minutes.
3. **Preheat Grill:**
    - Preheat your grill to medium-high heat.
4. **Grill Vegetables:**
    - Arrange vegetables in a single layer on the grill. Grill for 4-6 minutes per side, or until tender and charred. Cherry tomatoes may cook faster, so keep an eye on them.
5. **Serve:**
    - Transfer grilled vegetables to a serving platter. Garnish with fresh basil or parsley and serve with lemon wedges if desired.

Enjoy your colorful and flavorful Summer Grilled Vegetable Platter!

Fall Baked Apples with Cinnamon

Ingredients:

- 4 large apples (such as Honeycrisp, Gala, or Granny Smith)
- 1/4 cup brown sugar
- 1/4 cup chopped walnuts or pecans
- 1/4 cup raisins or dried cranberries
- 1/2 teaspoon ground cinnamon
- 1/4 teaspoon ground nutmeg
- 2 tablespoons unsalted butter, cut into small pieces
- 1/4 cup water or apple cider
- Vanilla ice cream or whipped cream (optional, for serving)

Instructions:

1. **Preheat Oven:**
    - Preheat your oven to 350°F (175°C).
2. **Prepare Apples:**
    - Core the apples, leaving the bottom intact to hold the filling. You can use an apple corer or a small knife to carefully remove the core.
3. **Mix Filling:**
    - In a small bowl, combine brown sugar, chopped nuts, raisins or cranberries, cinnamon, and nutmeg.
4. **Stuff Apples:**
    - Place the apples in a baking dish. Spoon the filling mixture into the center of each apple.
    - Top each apple with a small piece of butter.
5. **Add Liquid:**
    - Pour water or apple cider into the bottom of the baking dish. This will help steam the apples and keep them moist.
6. **Bake:**
    - Cover the baking dish with aluminum foil and bake for 25-30 minutes. Remove the foil and bake for an additional 10-15 minutes, or until the apples are tender when pierced with a fork.
7. **Serve:**
    - Let the apples cool slightly before serving. Serve warm with a scoop of vanilla ice cream or a dollop of whipped cream if desired.

Enjoy your cozy and aromatic Fall Baked Apples with Cinnamon!

Winter Spinach and Feta Stuffed Chicken

Ingredients:

- 4 boneless, skinless chicken breasts
- 2 cups fresh spinach, chopped
- 1/2 cup crumbled feta cheese
- 1/4 cup grated Parmesan cheese
- 2 cloves garlic, minced
- 1 tablespoon olive oil
- 1/2 teaspoon dried oregano
- 1/2 teaspoon dried thyme
- Salt and pepper, to taste
- Toothpicks or kitchen twine

Instructions:

1. **Preheat Oven:**
    - Preheat your oven to 375°F (190°C).
2. **Prepare Filling:**
    - In a skillet, heat olive oil over medium heat. Add garlic and cook for 1 minute until fragrant.
    - Add chopped spinach and cook until wilted. Remove from heat and let cool slightly.
    - In a bowl, combine spinach, feta cheese, and Parmesan cheese.
3. **Stuff Chicken:**
    - Place each chicken breast between two sheets of plastic wrap. Gently pound with a meat mallet or rolling pin until about 1/2 inch thick.
    - Spread the spinach and feta mixture evenly over each chicken breast.
    - Roll up each chicken breast tightly and secure with toothpicks or kitchen twine.
4. **Season and Bake:**
    - Season the outside of the chicken with salt, pepper, oregano, and thyme.
    - Place the stuffed chicken breasts in a baking dish and bake for 25-30 minutes, or until the chicken reaches an internal temperature of 165°F (74°C).
5. **Serve:**
    - Let the chicken rest for a few minutes before removing toothpicks or twine. Slice and serve warm.

Enjoy your flavorful and satisfying Winter Spinach and Feta Stuffed Chicken!

Spring Roasted Lemon Herb Chicken

Ingredients:

- 1 whole chicken (about 4-5 lbs), patted dry
- 2 lemons, quartered
- 4 cloves garlic, minced
- 3 tablespoons olive oil
- 1 tablespoon fresh rosemary, chopped (or 1 teaspoon dried)
- 1 tablespoon fresh thyme, chopped (or 1 teaspoon dried)
- Salt and pepper, to taste
- Fresh herbs for garnish (optional)

Instructions:

1. **Preheat Oven:**
    - Preheat your oven to 425°F (220°C).
2. **Prepare Chicken:**
    - Rub the chicken all over with olive oil. Season generously with salt and pepper.
    - Stuff the cavity with lemon quarters and a few sprigs of rosemary and thyme.
3. **Season and Roast:**
    - Rub minced garlic and remaining herbs all over the chicken.
    - Place the chicken breast side up on a rack in a roasting pan.
    - Roast for 1 to 1.5 hours, or until the internal temperature reaches 165°F (74°C) and the skin is golden and crispy.
4. **Rest and Serve:**
    - Let the chicken rest for 10 minutes before carving.
    - Garnish with additional fresh herbs if desired and serve with the roasted lemon quarters.

Enjoy your bright and flavorful Spring Roasted Lemon Herb Chicken!

Summer Thai Beef Salad

Ingredients:

- **For the Salad:**
    - 1 lb (450 g) beef sirloin or flank steak
    - 4 cups mixed salad greens (like lettuce, spinach, or arugula)
    - 1 cup cherry tomatoes, halved
    - 1 cucumber, thinly sliced
    - 1/2 red onion, thinly sliced
    - 1/2 cup fresh cilantro, chopped
    - 1/4 cup fresh mint leaves, chopped
    - 1/4 cup chopped peanuts or cashews (optional)
- **For the Dressing:**
    - 1/4 cup lime juice (about 2 limes)
    - 2 tablespoons fish sauce
    - 1 tablespoon soy sauce
    - 1 tablespoon brown sugar or honey
    - 1 clove garlic, minced
    - 1 small red chili, finely chopped (optional, for heat)

Instructions:

1. **Cook the Beef:**
    - Season the beef with salt and pepper. Grill or sear in a hot pan over medium-high heat for about 4-5 minutes per side, or until desired doneness. Let it rest for 5 minutes before slicing thinly against the grain.
2. **Prepare the Dressing:**
    - In a small bowl, whisk together lime juice, fish sauce, soy sauce, brown sugar or honey, minced garlic, and chopped chili if using.
3. **Assemble the Salad:**
    - In a large bowl, combine salad greens, cherry tomatoes, cucumber, red onion, cilantro, and mint.
    - Add the sliced beef and toss with the dressing.
4. **Garnish and Serve:**
    - Sprinkle with chopped peanuts or cashews if desired.

Enjoy your fresh and flavorful Summer Thai Beef Salad!

Fall Acorn Squash with Maple Glaze

Ingredients:

- 2 acorn squash
- 2 tablespoons olive oil
- 1/4 cup pure maple syrup
- 1 tablespoon balsamic vinegar
- 1/2 teaspoon ground cinnamon
- 1/4 teaspoon ground nutmeg
- Salt and pepper, to taste
- Fresh thyme or parsley for garnish (optional)

Instructions:

1. **Preheat Oven:**
   - Preheat your oven to 400°F (200°C).
2. **Prepare Squash:**
   - Cut each acorn squash in half and scoop out the seeds.
   - Brush the cut sides with olive oil and season with salt and pepper.
3. **Roast Squash:**
   - Place the squash halves cut-side down on a baking sheet.
   - Roast for 25-30 minutes, or until tender.
4. **Prepare Maple Glaze:**
   - While the squash is roasting, in a small bowl, mix maple syrup, balsamic vinegar, cinnamon, and nutmeg.
5. **Glaze and Finish:**
   - After 25-30 minutes, flip the squash halves cut-side up.
   - Brush or drizzle the maple glaze over the squash.
   - Roast for an additional 10-15 minutes, or until the glaze is caramelized and the squash is tender.
6. **Serve:**
   - Garnish with fresh thyme or parsley if desired.

Enjoy your sweet and savory Fall Acorn Squash with Maple Glaze!

Winter Sweet Potato Shepherd's Pie

Ingredients:

- **For the Sweet Potato Topping:**
    - 4 large sweet potatoes, peeled and cubed
    - 2 tablespoons unsalted butter
    - 1/4 cup milk or cream
    - Salt and pepper, to taste
- **For the Meat Filling:**
    - 1 lb (450 g) ground beef or lamb
    - 1 onion, chopped
    - 2 cloves garlic, minced
    - 2 carrots, diced
    - 1 cup frozen peas
    - 1 tablespoon tomato paste
    - 1 cup beef or vegetable broth
    - 1 teaspoon dried thyme
    - 1 teaspoon dried rosemary
    - Salt and pepper, to taste

Instructions:

1. **Prepare Sweet Potatoes:**
    - Boil sweet potatoes in a large pot of salted water until tender, about 15 minutes. Drain well.
    - Mash the sweet potatoes with butter and milk until smooth. Season with salt and pepper. Set aside.
2. **Cook the Meat Filling:**
    - In a large skillet, cook the ground beef or lamb over medium heat until browned. Drain excess fat.
    - Add onion and garlic, cooking until softened, about 5 minutes.
    - Stir in carrots and cook for another 5 minutes.
    - Add tomato paste and cook for 1 minute.
    - Pour in the broth and add thyme, rosemary, salt, and pepper. Simmer for 10 minutes, or until the mixture thickens slightly. Stir in frozen peas.
3. **Assemble the Pie:**
    - Preheat your oven to 375°F (190°C).
    - Spread the meat filling in the bottom of a baking dish.
    - Spoon the mashed sweet potatoes over the top, spreading evenly.
4. **Bake:**
    - Bake for 25-30 minutes, or until the top is slightly browned and the filling is bubbling.
5. **Serve:**

- Let the pie cool for a few minutes before serving.

Enjoy your hearty and flavorful Winter Sweet Potato Shepherd's Pie!

Spring Chickpea and Avocado Salad

Ingredients:

- **For the Salad:**
    - 1 can (15 oz) chickpeas, drained and rinsed
    - 1 ripe avocado, diced
    - 1 cup cherry tomatoes, halved
    - 1 cucumber, diced
    - 1/4 red onion, finely chopped
    - 1/4 cup fresh parsley or cilantro, chopped
- **For the Dressing:**
    - 3 tablespoons olive oil
    - 2 tablespoons lemon juice (about 1 lemon)
    - 1 clove garlic, minced
    - 1 teaspoon Dijon mustard
    - 1/2 teaspoon ground cumin
    - Salt and pepper, to taste

Instructions:

1. **Prepare the Vegetables:**
    - In a large bowl, combine chickpeas, avocado, cherry tomatoes, cucumber, red onion, and fresh parsley or cilantro.
2. **Make the Dressing:**
    - In a small bowl or jar, whisk together olive oil, lemon juice, minced garlic, Dijon mustard, ground cumin, salt, and pepper.
3. **Combine:**
    - Pour the dressing over the salad and toss gently to coat all the ingredients.
4. **Serve:**
    - Serve immediately, or chill in the refrigerator for up to 1 hour before serving to let the flavors meld.

Enjoy your bright and nutritious Spring Chickpea and Avocado Salad!

Summer Strawberry Shortcake

Ingredients:

- **For the Strawberries:**
    - 4 cups fresh strawberries, hulled and sliced
    - 1/4 cup granulated sugar
- **For the Shortcakes:**
    - 2 cups all-purpose flour
    - 1/4 cup granulated sugar
    - 1 tablespoon baking powder
    - 1/2 teaspoon salt
    - 1/2 cup cold unsalted butter, cubed
    - 3/4 cup milk
    - 1 teaspoon vanilla extract
- **For the Whipped Cream:**
    - 1 cup heavy cream
    - 2 tablespoons powdered sugar
    - 1 teaspoon vanilla extract

Instructions:

1. **Prepare Strawberries:**
    - In a bowl, toss the sliced strawberries with 1/4 cup sugar. Let them sit for at least 30 minutes to release their juices.
2. **Make Shortcakes:**
    - Preheat oven to 425°F (220°C).
    - In a large bowl, whisk together flour, sugar, baking powder, and salt.
    - Cut in the cold butter until the mixture resembles coarse crumbs.
    - Stir in milk and vanilla until just combined.
    - Turn dough onto a floured surface and gently knead. Pat to about 1-inch thickness and cut into rounds with a biscuit cutter.
    - Place on a baking sheet and bake for 12-15 minutes, or until golden brown. Let cool.
3. **Prepare Whipped Cream:**
    - In a chilled bowl, beat heavy cream with powdered sugar and vanilla extract until soft peaks form.
4. **Assemble:**
    - Slice the shortcakes in half. Spoon strawberries over the bottom half, add a dollop of whipped cream, and top with the other half of the shortcake.

Enjoy your light and refreshing Summer Strawberry Shortcake!

www.ingramcontent.com/pod-product-compliance
Lightning Source LLC
LaVergne TN
LVHW061946070526
838199LV00060B/3999